Forms and Shades

Bruce Pratt

Poems by Bruce Pratt
Clare Songbirds Publishing House Poetry Series
ISBN 978-1-947653-45-0
Clare Songbirds Publishing House
Forms and Shades © 2019 Bruce Pratt

All Rights Reserved. Clare Songbirds Publishing House retains right to reprint.
Permission to reprint individual poems must be obtained from the author who owns the copyright.

Printed in the United States of America
FIRST EDITION

Clare Songbirds Publishing House Mission Statement:
Clare Songbirds Publishing House was established to provide a print forum for the creation of limited edition, fine art from poets and writers, both established and emerging. We strive to reignite and continue a tradition of quality, accessible literary arts to the national and international community of writers, and readers. Chapbook manuscripts are carefully chosen for their ability to propel the expansion of art and ideas in literary form. We provide an accessible way to promote the art of words in order to resonate with, and impact, readers not yet familiar with the siren song of poets and writers. Clare Songbirds Publishing House espouses a singular cultural development where poetry creates community and becomes commonplace in public places.

140 Cottage Street
Auburn, New York 13021
www.claresongbirdspub.com

CONTENTS

Sonnets and Villavariations

Love at the Darkening of the Day	7
I Know Why a Man	8
December Morning	9
A Quarrel of Crows	10
A Distant Ship Tiding Home	11
According to as Spokesman	12
Think of Sophia Loren	13
September's Last Afternoon	14
Villanelle for Patrick	15
I Cursed Neither the Gods Nor The Moon	16
The Rectitude of the April Wind	17
The Sound of Darkness	18
Follow Me Through Night Streets	19
Rain Dimples the Pond	20

A Newfoundland Suite   21

Shades

Interpreting Her Dreams	31
A Grosbeak in *The Simmer Dim*	32
Angel in the Window	33
Scar	34
Dialing it In	35
In This Winter of Stingy Snow and Illness	36
Sunday Morning Poaching	37

The following poems appeared in these journals, reviews, collections and anthologies sometimes in slightly different forms.

"According to a Spokesman," *Veils, Halos, and Shackles: International Poetry on the Oppression and Empowerment of Women*. Kasva Press 2016 Fishman and Sahay Eds., *Poet's Touchstone 2007, and Boreal,* Antrim House Books 2007

"A distant ship tiding home," *Ellipsis* 2007, and in *Boreal* Antrim House Books 2007.

"A Grosbeak in the Simmer Dim," and "Rain Dimples the Pond," *Tipton Poetry Journal* 2017

"Angel in the Window," *Northern New England Review* 2010

"A Quarrel of Crows," *Red Rock Review* 2007, B*oreal Antrim House Books* 2007, and *Villanelles, Everyman's Library Pocket Poets,* Alfred Knopf New York. Eds. Finch and Elizabeth-Mali.

"December Morning," *Off The Coast,* 2008

"Dialing it In," *Sin Fronteras* 2010

"Interpreting Her Dream," *Smartish Pace* 2007

"Sunday Poaching," *Naugatuck Review* 2010

"Think of Sophia Loren," *Stolen Island Review* 2015

dedication

Love at the Darkening of the Day

Echoes of Christmas lie exhausted, now mute and still,
Like children fatigued from the day's clattered racket,
As weary December light pales and dips behind Doc's hill—
The western sky dark an hour before official sunset.

The dying year points toward the sun, pauses as if rested,
And before the last calendar page is torn from the wall
Holds hard in its memory that love eternally tested.
For love reborn at the darkening of a day knows no Fall.

The birches have in harsh, sinuous shadows snaked
Across the moon's light, pine crowns have ceased their sway,
As the wind, too, lies spent on the mountainside, bedded
Down with the huddled deer, unstirring, until the new day
Grasps in its infant hands the rising face of the sun,
And holds it to its chest against our star's solstice run.

I Know Why a Man.
for Janet on her Birthday

I know why a man yearns to wander land of his own,
to amble among kindred orchard, field, maple grove,
marking his and another's not by fence, wall, or gate,
but the stream's bend, the intersection of abandoned roads.

I know why a man seeks solace in singing spring fields,
wades amid the waving waist-high hay of waning summer,
lies down as colors riot to know the earth's last warmth,
rambles with gun and dog in rasping grasses of November.

And I know why a man takes a woman to be his lover,
to wake with to the antiphonal airs of May warblers,
to tangle with in the damp heat of moonstruck July covers,
to cleave to when rising Orion girds his belted cynosure,
to calm in the bleak, storm-sung rage of dark December,
and to cobble the stubborn griefs of their sorrows together.

December Morning

How bone hard the block of suet must be
that the downy batters between the feeder bars,
after a cloudless night of moon-dimmed stars
the mercury plunged to minus three,

before first rays have mounted the dark trees,
banished the glow of the morning star's light
and hiked the ashy hem of the fading night,
waking woodpeckers and blizzards of chickadees.

I stir steel cut oats and maple syrup, grade A,
steep dark coffee in the press, sip it black,
settle in my chair, the woodstove at my back,
pleasing my tongue in this still dark hour of day.

Summoned by hunger, the crow's quarrelsome caw,
Dawn staggers in the roséd east, sullen and raw.

A Quarrel of Crows

A quarrel of crows
glean treasure from torn trash bags
on a rural road,

strut and cakewalk with
raspy-throated posturing.
A quarrel of crows

strip away limp gray rind
like coyotes feasting on doe.
On a rural road,

coon-toppled barrels,
bequeath uneaten orts to
a quarrel of crows

who caw, grateful for
this desiccated banquet
on a rural road.

On the first Friday
of the last month of the year,
a quarrel of crows
on a rural road.

A Distant Ship Tiding Home

A distant ship tiding home,
reefed against mad easterlies,
tacks north past a bare headland.

Surf swarms a widow's ankles,
sand and prayer surging seaward.
A distant ship tiding home,

heeling in haste to her rail,
chases her salt-flecked bowsprit,
tacks north past a bare headland.

Quarreling east wind and storm tide
roil the gravid sea, savage
a distant ship tiding home,

lash the widow's gathered skirts.
Sails vanished, her harrowed hope
tacks north past a bare headland.

Wind, a murmur of women,
cursing tide, singing shingles.
A distant ship tiding home
tacks north past a bare headland.

According to a Spokesman

Raped, beaten, and thrown down an embankment,
left by her three male attackers for dead,
her injuries are not life threatening.

The name of the victim has been withheld.
A man notified police as she was being
raped, beaten, and thrown down an embankment,

that he had been in the car with the woman
when his friends planned to assault and kill her.
Her injuries are not life threatening,

and the caller is credited with saving the victim's life
by leading medical personnel to where she was
raped, beaten, and thrown down an embankment.

The caller identified two of the suspects.
Another was found hiding under a bench.
Her injuries are not life threatening.

She should recover fully from her ordeal,
according to a hospital spokesman, because though
raped, beaten, and thrown down an embankment
her injuries are not life threatening.

Think of Sophia Loren

Listen to cellos
while eating a ripe Bosc pear.
Think of Sophia Loren.

Taste the both of them,
one *dolce*, one perfect salt.
Listen to cellos,

imagine your bow
drawn across her thigh's tendons.
Think of Sophia Loren,

music coaxed from flesh,
life commingling in fluid.
Listen to cellos,

argue with the wind,
of impossibilities.
Think of Sophia Loren,

as Dulcinea,
a beauty at seventy.
Listen to cellos.
Think of Sophia Loren.

September's Last Afternoon

September's last afternoon,
color sparks the ridge.
A child paints outside the lines.

Wind coughs in stubbled hayfields
ringed by blue asters.
September's last afternoon,

tire flattened crab apples
fester with yellow jackets.
A child paints outside the lines,

yellow sun fused to brown field,
red tree, opaque cloud.
September's last afternoon

limps toward a hard frost.
Orion's blood surges.
A child paints outside the lines,

and God has drunk far too much
staring beauty down.
September's last afternoon.
A child painting outside the lines.

Villanelle for Patrick
in memory of Patrick Sullivan

Ireland's map graced his face,
as humble as her patron saint,
music and decency rose in his blood.

Born of gentle people, a strong soul,
stranger to indifference or hate,
Ireland's map graced his face,

Connemara rain on greening fields,
sun shadows slanting Slieve Liag.
Music and decency rose in his blood,

bequeathed him melody and song,
the mysteries of frets and strings.
Ireland's map graced his face,

he intuited in her history of hunger
the fulfillment of feeding others.
Music and decency rose in his blood,

bold as the bodhran's taut tattoo,
soft as a slow air through Uillean pipes.
Ireland's map graced his face,
music and decency rose in his blood.

I Cursed Neither The Gods Nor The Moon
for Elizabeth Wilkins Lombardo

I cursed neither the gods nor the moon,
nor raged the length of grieved night,
because Beth would not wish us to.

My soul steeped in despair's sin,
roared against dividing cells, but
I cursed neither the gods nor the moon,

did not ponder why I survived and
one so much worthier did not,
because Beth would not wish us to,

rive our hearts with pity and anger,
or converse in the language of war.
I cursed neither the gods nor the moon,

nor howled a lament into the dark,
asking why no one teaches us how to die
because Beth would not wish us to.

I could not dam the salty rivers,
nor calm my quaking heart, but
I cursed neither the gods nor the moon,
because Beth would not wish us to.

The Rectitude of the April Wind

The rectitude of the April wind
punishes snow in the windrows,
exhorting winter to concede,

and melt into the greening fields,
to pause and pledge fealty to
the rectitude of the April wind,

that natters in the naked maples,
and brays in the barren birches,
exhorting winter to concede,

as morning hounds the hoar frost,
and afternoon waits to set, as
the rectitude of the April wind

orders the dark cedar groves
to yield to the rising light,
exhorting winter to concede,

and frenzied flocks of finches zip
from leafless wild roses on
the rectitude of the April wind,
exhorting winter to concede.

The Sound of Darkness

The sound of darkness,
sifted through frozen fingers,
exhales memory,

a bed of north wind,
sheets of hail and rusted rain.
The sound of darkness

protests in dead leaves,
discovers dawn's hiding place,
exhales memory

into nascent light,
ghosting, rising, lost to air.
The sound of darkness,

stripped of harmony
laments the cruel idle moon,
exhales memory,

insomniac wind,
the oracle's blind moaning.
The sound of darkness
exhales memory.

Follow Me Through Night Streets

Follow me through night streets,
Beyond the pale of village light,
Beneath naked October trees,

Where sky and mountain meet,
In the diaspora of the night.
Follow me through night streets,

Sleet elegies sung on the breeze,
Invisible to rising Orion's sight.
Beneath naked October trees,

When in their tongues the dead speak
From their side of Samhain's night,
Follow me through night streets,

The season's departed souls to greet,
As the old year wanes from sight,
Beneath naked October trees.

Tir na nOg's voices haunt the breeze,
Sounding lullabies across the night,
Follow me through night streets,
Beneath naked October trees.

Rain Dimples the Pond
for Kathleen Ellis

Rain dimples the pond,
blackbird lights on a cattail,
dusk of high summer.

Murmurs of thunder,
caress the beaver's dark wake.
Rain dimples the pond,

quilts of purple clouds,
lightning south over the bay.
Dusk of high summer,

chickadees burst from,
white petals of mock orange.
Rain dimples the pond,

bold goldfinches sway,
on the sunflower feeders,
dusk of high summer.

The wind swings northwest,
storm crawling toward the sea,
rain dimples the pond,
dusk of high summer.

A Newfoundland Suite

I.
Eventide
evening
night's embryo
fusses and tosses
stretching cramped limbs
kneading knotted muscle
desperate for rest
or impulse

butt end rings of day's haze
runic in the sea breeze
kiss gently on dim wave caps
read without language or stone
dimming day yielded
to

tide and wind surge
rising star
setting sun
obdurate moon

desire stiffens
the breeze slacks
old love
Gnostic
practiced
smooth as beach glass

rubbed with time
nubbled
at the edges of arousal

in the sea's house
rock and slosh
seminal secrets

on the beach
glyphs
ephemeral sentences
read between tides
sing of the ancients
created there
in the thigh locked
calling

the dream begins
always
with the whispers of dark

susurrus
in the waves
blown into the ear
tumid
scented with kelp
salt
sweat
sand
cod bones
flensed flesh of whale
bikini skin

spindrift
souls spit back from the sea
eyes devoured by fish
seaweed riots of hair

bonfires
cannot burn
down
into the
sand
like the dusty humus of the dry woods
and wait only for the tide
to crack their
ring of stones and drown their ardor
a careless stern man
caught in his rope.

day does not settle for
evening's caesura
night
pulses behind the
falling sun
a predator
who accepts carrion
when
no other meal presents itself

harridan winds
scour the dunes
drive west wind
against the tide
swell a gravid sea
harrow hearts
with nightmare and
insomnia
breeze
births
a quiet dawn

froth-tongued
bell hung
waves
lullabies
of
death's
second self
salubrious seductions
from woe-fraught
daylight
hush and stroke
us to our bower and
release

dark
as porous as the sea
vexed by starlight
gossamer as
spindrift
distant as noon
inky cloak of
rest
droops over the
beds and cots
of the restless
leg and aching loins
cover
for the
rush and tatter of labor
reflection.

The cod's cerements,
rise on graceful grey swells
fog-choked and tide-borne

dissolve in mute spindrift,
against the rock-templed shore.
The cod's cerements

spit from trawler's nets
sing dirges beyond man's ken
fog-choked and tide-borne,

psalms sung in fish tongues
complaints to the moon and Gods
The cod's cerements

leach into shingle
to be buried by the flood
fog-choked and tide-borne

East wind calls the rain
north wind calls clearing and
the cod's cerements
fog-choked and tide-borne

II.
Night's House

mustard sun and
aluminum moon
suck wind
from the tide's mouth

stilled sea at
dimmed day

waves spasm
air crackling
current surges
in night's house
tangling bolts
in the
beach dwellers hearts
singeing reason
searing the
salt wet skin
and sanctified souls of
of the tide and
murmuring
fish

a finger of fog
beckons
be a passerby

write no epistles in
the sand or wind
of your bone

sculpt a sand bed
carve each curve

a word

dispel weariness
slay struggle
misshape
the mayhem of
ineluctable light

imprison the distraction
of morning

rise

stand with the silence
snared in your fingers

knit the skeins of
night
into a cloak
for the eyes

fall

baleen odes
whistled through whale's teeth
threnody and dirge
drown the waves
of a pockmarked
sea
as exhausted as
the loins of a whore

dolmen breakers
portals
a birth sluice
first crawling over
the cooled sand
settling ooze
great seepings
in the
ebony
omnipresence of
grunt and squeal

tactile blindness
a newborn bat
echolocating
star and moon
triangulating
parameters of existence
in the pocket
of a dream

thunder
quaking isobars
ridged sea
blown back
goosefleshed
damp tangle of sheet

and leg
aching for the wind
to back
barometer to rise
into the
star house

after the rocking
a child quiets
raspy-breathed
febrile
to her mother's touch
scorching her breast
with heat and hurt
prone between
progenitors
in the musty percale
of the storm
heavy
night bed

dreaming
in the drip of the eaves
a rhythm of sleep

the sea slaps the land
for thieving her pulse
with its wind

fired across a continent
abated now as the tide
neaps

the mother remembers her child's
cry
not her creating

in the exhaustion of clouds
empyrean fire
light
like slits in a mask
of mute darkness
thunder

In staggering dark
baroque motets spiral on
spirit-drunk voices,

abrade ancient stone
like water sundering slate.
In staggering dark

the penitent's peace
is lit by lambent tapers.
Spirit-drunk voices,

the prayers of the maimed,
nettle Darwin's hoary beard.
In staggering dark,

Crom's atavistic
winter-bleak fear conjures the
spirit-drunk voices,

curses the meadow
bathed in shadows and lost shades.
In staggering dark,
spirit-drunk voices.

III
Dawn's Cave
province of bird
wearied nocturnal hunter
riots of insect
and half dream
of chanting whales
absent of wind

whisper to fatigued night
seducing it to
surrender
heave of tide
swallowed sea wrack
moon-sipped morning

summoned from ebon heavens

the land exhales
sunlight stirring the wind
dune grass shivers
silicas of spent rock
collapsed in whorls

where the plover pecks at
bleached exoskeletons
gorged up from the sea
day glints
a match in a sconce

a woman timid before
a new lover

a man
fearsome before a mirror
of water

sea inhales
earth damp wind
flung from
dunes and cliffs
humid as a dog's breath
redolent as spent
lovers' sweat
evaporating before
the breeze
luffing in the curtains
like penitents praying
before
a bitter god
confessing ineluctable
stumbles
of resolution

moon tide
in the dripping eaves
long after the sun
has whitened the sand

ringing halyards in the
weather helm
moorings stretched
like a crane's neck

beyond the banked fog
bronzed men
shiver
bait slicks
slither
in the wake
coiled lines pay out
traps sink and
hope rises
like bile in the gorge
of a saint

obdurate gray insistent
like the smoke of
flaming forests
morning demands
attention
banishes stars and moon
pesters dewy sedge
lashes toil

from the
boughs of
the night bed
surly stilettos of light
shaming the supine
supplicating
storming
harridan
and harbinger

light spattered
tide-abandoned
rails against
the moon
withdrawing from
the shore
its night growl
suffused in whisper

snap of canvas
diesel-throated clouds
arc of sinker
trail of bait
a splash beyond the foam
where fish argue
about deceit and intent.

throb of hurricane bone
energy waves
sprinting from Africa
eye
sheared away by cousin winds
but unblinking
stalwart
engorged on
warm water
scout swells
tremors across wave crests
prescient squalls
regains vision
scans the coast for
landfall
fields to drench
limbs to murder
dreams to drown
silt to salt the sea.

light
the pock
of wind lashed sea
the instant of

no tide
beach and sedge
rest
stretches her limbs
wrings salt from
dendritic tresses
rubs her bruised thighs
traces
sand caked
ravines in her face
remembering
the banshee scream
of the
gale's fury
moan
of
regret
leaking
new death
heralded in gull screech

In the insistence of light
mourning is vanquished
slain like frost before high sun

inevitable morning
as night's specters, hushed
In the insistence of light

gravity, elegy of spin
torture dreams of flight
slain like frost before high sun

Wind bares brittle branches
clacks salutes to the tide
in the insistence of light

that pales by the planet's tilt
toward darker hours,
like frost before high sun

spirit drunk voices
like the old cod's cerements
in the insistence of light
like frost before high sun

Interpreting Her Dream

a dawning disquietude
of half-heard birds,

mumbled away grunting
in alchemy and vision.

scribbled along her forehead
the hieroglyphs of the dream.

rain surging back to snow,
wind backing to the north,

startled snores and half words
snagged between Eros and terror,

flexing and releasing of muscle
imbedded in the mind's knot,

straining to name a name.

A Grosbeak in *The Simmer Dim*

When I pass this time,
I should prefer to return
as a male, rose-breasted
grosbeak, who frequents
a window feeder at a
house like mine, where
an aging couple thinks
I'm handsome, and
never begrudge me a
daily scoop of black
oil sunflower seeds,
discarded hulls littering
their flowerbeds,
in the long lilac-scented
evenings of late June—
the time the Orkney and
Shetland Scots call
The Simmer Dim,
that light of reflection
whiskey and kinship,
that migrates away
before the birds.

Angel in The Window

The display segued from Christmas to Valentine's Day,
as if there was nothing in between to celebrate with a sale.

For two months the angel had hovered over the animals,
gazing down on the manger. Mary knelt beside Joseph

who stood mute and rigid, hands at his side, allowing the
motley robed Magi to pose with their tribute for the child.

The angel kept her halo after her nippleless chest and
hairless mons were cinched into a velvet bustier and garters,

her pale skin glowing in the fluorescent light, resplendent in red,
taller in her stilettos, rotated a quarter turn to the street.

Expression unchanged, mouth slightly ajar, chin steady,
left hand beckoning, I swear I saw the flutter of her wings.

Scar

A fly hovers over
    tea-colored water
        at Thor Ballylee,
Like Maud's image
    frozen in the agony
        of Yeats's scar.
Lighting on the surface
    near the rise,
        it is ignored.
Where the tower's shadow
    meets the rippling line
        of the noonday sun,
My false casts snap like a whip.

Dialing it In

She's honed the skills of living single,
pricking her soul on those blades
until she no longer hits a nerve,
or notices the skin parting
across the surface of her heart.

Drip only enough Lemon Joy
onto the sponge to clean,
knife, fork, plate, nonstick pan,
and to wipe the counter where
the chicken breast thawed.

Pump the air out
of the half-drained bottle of
French cabernet, to sustain its
warmth for dinner or
the depths of the next night.

Keep a book going for when blizzards
and thunderstorms knock out the cable,
or for when one hundred and sixty stations
and forty pay per view channels
are simply not enough.

Never drink and dial anyone,
not him, your mother, best friend;
keep the phone buried in your purse
until summoned by the ring tone of
"Happy Days Are Here Again."

Then, answer only on the third ring
after checking the caller ID
to ensure that no one else's despair
is waiting for you to pick up
to harrow the soft spot in your soul.

In This Winter of Stingy Snow and Illnesses

In this winter of stingy snow and illnesses,
we have nursed each other as we may in old age,

not by necessity but of love, the kind,
which born in us, does not wither like

the dirtied banks beside the muddied road,
sun struck and singing in the ditches,

nor dissipate like the grey clouds flattening
Katahdin's distant white summits,

but endures like granite beneath the ridge.

Sunday Morning Poaching

We pilfer a dark stroll
a few minutes before six
along a damp manicured fairway,
does grazing in nervous shadows,
grouse exploding from the rough,
poachers, non-members, like us.

With our ancient dog, unable to
detect or menace these interlopers,
we have encroached from the woods
near the third tee, obscured from
the gaze of the hungover pro smoking
his morning joint by the caddy shack.

Sprinklers hiss, a mower drones,
a heron glides into the shallows of
the misted water hazard where I've
fished in moon flung midnight,
for slack water, bleary-eyed bass,
and fertilizer stunned blue gills.

A great blue heron stalks the reedy
edges of the pond for toxic frogs, and
I recall the susurrus September night
I cast a number six brown popper
into a sinuous shaft of moonglow
and landed a four-pound largemouth.

A scimitar reflected in the brown
and green ripples of the silted pond,
he arced in three jaw-shaking leaps,
but as I had no net, and no one waiting,
I played him until he went slack,
then hauled him onto the dew slick grass.

Unable to revive him, I slit his belly,
full of dead grandchildren, a tangle of black
insects, and a yellow Dunlop range ball
with a split lip crease, imprisoned like
a giant, decomposing salmon egg
or a child awaiting her Caesarian birth.

Bruce Pratt edits *American Fiction*, for which he won the Midwest Independent Publishers Association's Gold Medal for Volume 13 and is the past Director of the *Northern Writes Project* at Penobscot Theatre Company in Bangor Maine. He graduated from Franklin and Marshall College with a BA in Religious Studies in 1973, The University of Maine with an MA in English with a concentration in Creative Writing in 2001, and The University of Southern Maine's Stonecoast MFA in 2004 with a degree in creative writing. He and his wife, Janet, live in Swanville Maine.

A 2008 Pushcart Award nominee, Pratt's novel, *The Serpents of Blissfull*, was published by Mountain State Press in 2011, and his short story collection *The Trash Detail* was published in 2018 by New Rivers Press. He won the 2007 *Andre Dubus Award*, and was a runner up or finalist for the 2007 fiction award from *Georgetown Review*, the 2007 flash fiction prize from *Mindprints*, the 2006 Ontario Prize, the 2005 Rick DeMarinis Short Story Award, and the 2003 Fiction Award from *Dogwood*. His short fiction has also appeared in *The Greensboro Review*, *The Boston Fiction Annual Review*, *The Dos Passos Review*, *WordSmitten Quarterly Journal*, *Briar Cliff Review*, *Portland Magazine*, *Watchword*, *The Staccato Literary Magazine*, *The Gihon River Review*, *The Dalhousie*

Review, Puckerbrush Review, Cooweescoowee, Existere, Vermont Literary Review, Hawk and Handsaw, The Blue Earth Review, Diner, Roanoke Review, Potomac Review, The Wisconsin Review, The Platte Valley Review, The Binnacle, Apocalypse, Crosscut, Stolen Island Review, and The Trust and Treachery Anthology.

Pratt's poetry collection *Boreal* is available from Antrim House Book. He was the winner of the 2007 *Ellipsis Prize* in poetry, a finalist for the Erskine J. Poetry award from *Smartish Pace*, and his poems have appeared in: *The Book of Villanelles* from Knopf's Everyman Series, the anthology *Only Connect*, (Cinnamon Press, Wales) *Veils, Halos and Shackles, International Poetry on the Oppression and Empowerment of Women*, (Kasva Press) *Smartish Pace, Revival* (Ireland), *Puckerbrush Review, The Hiram Poetry Review The Naugatuck Review, The Poet's Touchstone, Rock and Sling, Red Rock Review, Iguana Review, Sin Fronteras, The Tipton Journal, Crosscut, The Unrorean, Heartland Review, Wild Goose Poetry Review* and *The Goose River Anthology*.

Pratt's nonfiction has appeared in *The Truth About The Fact Anthology, Yale Anglers' Journal, Vermont Literary Review, The Hartford Courant, Bangor Daily News, Salty Dog, Bangor Metro*, and *Portland Magazine*.

His short play *Electrolysis* was performed at the 2008 Maine Short Play Festival and was included in the 2nd Annual Northern Writes Festival, and his short play *Polygamy* appeared in *Literal Latte* in 2009. *Barter* a one-act was included in the 2010 Maine Play Festival and The Northern Writes Festival, where it won an audience choice award. *Wednesday?* was featured in the 2010 0-60 Longwood Play Festival in Virginia, and Words and Wine in New York City. *Beaching*, a ten-minute play was part of the 2011 Northern Writes Festival and won the audience choice award. *Schubert's Monkey* was one of three short plays chosen for the 2012 Northern Writes New Works Festival, and *Memories of Paradise* appeared in *Aethlon: The Journal of Sport Literature*, and in the 2013 Maine Play Festival. His play full-length play *The King of France* won the 2016 Meetinghouse Theatre Lab's play competition, and his full length play *Radio Silent* won the same award in 2017. In August 2018 the same group will present some of his own-act plays.

www.ingramcontent.com/pod-product-compliance
Lightning Source LLC
Chambersburg PA
CBHW030142100526
44592CB00011B/1005